Politics of the Minotaur

Politics of the Minotaur

Poems

karla k. morton

Texas Review Press

Huntsville, Texas

Published by Texas Review Press
Huntsville, Texas 77341
texasreviewpress.org

Printed in the United States of America

Library of Congress Cataloging in Publication Data
is on file at the Library of Congress, Washington, DC

Cover photo: "Minotaur and Ariadne" by Federico Severino, photograph by karla k. morton. Used with permission of the artist.

Cover and Interior Design: Bradley Alan Ivey

Contents

Kindness

I know you felt it—
that moment it slipped into your voice
like a foot
to a favorite shoe;

There there, you crooned, *It's all good.*

When you looked down to see
your mother's hands,
your father's knuckles;

when your arms reached out
to guide, to lift, to steady,
to pull another to your chest—
heart so close to heart;

the immediate flood of senses
when you realized
compassion is not pity;
that everything under the chariot sun
is made to green and strengthen
and feed each other;

that we are all flawed and bent—
frailty, our second shoe.

That a horrid mess is just a mess
and *everything* can be cleaned.

And when we lean our heads back
and open our mouths to the flood of song,

the notes join hands
above us,
and we become something
without edge or boundary;
something vast and winged;

a talaria
even the golden gods
cannot contain.

Politics of the Minotaur

In the fireplace,
whispers of Lakota ghosts
wander the embers;
the murmur and prickle of voices,
the heavy chant of hooves;

a great sadness risen 100 years
like this burning tree,
its round log—a splintered hoop,

labyrinth lines
seared in and out of the bark;

a people with no clew
to set themselves free,
guilty only of an existence
another wanted;
the politics of the Minotaur.

So they ride the Oomaka Tokatakiya
to wipe the tears of seven generations,
clinging to the thread of leather reigns

knowing there is still a beast to be conquered—

his steaming nostrils,
his naked tips of horns.

Arlington Cemetery, Washington D.C.

—for Alex "Sandy" Cathro

There is no synonym for Quagga, I muse,
as I watch the funeral procession.

Quagga, that extinct breed of African equine
with stripes at its head and shoulders.

These six that carry the military casket,
dappled—more white than grey,
blunt cut blonde tails;
straight backed at attention;
one without rider.

Here we feel the *olde* world,
the endangered species
of horse and carriage;
of bells that lick the metal hours;
of soldiers still serving
beneath draped flags and chiseled stones.

A colonel once told me
life was simple in the military—
Reveille every morning,
Taps every night.

There was routine and precision and purpose;
rules for chaos;
provisions even for death:

one flag with thirteen folds,
one rectangular ration of white granite,
one horse with empty saddle
to cumber,
to canter
its long legs of loss.

In the Arsenic Pool

Men always seem to notice it first,
What kind of stone is that?

Lapis.
The stone that relieves headaches,
the stone preferred over gold
by Cleopatra,
the stone on my middle finger,
once worn on RC Gorman's pinky.

I can't explain my attraction—
perhaps the perfect hypnotic blue,
the specks of pyrite,
the heavy knuckle of silver.

In the arsenic pool,
men gathered around it,
the rusty hot springs
glistening its cerulean hues,
gold veins capturing sunset.

Some kind of healing happened
in that Ojo Caliente,
vibes of a great artist
electrifying the waters,

arsenic drawing out toxins
leftover in our bodies
from chemo
and stroke
and stock market poverty,

and me in the middle,
new hair
black as an Egyptian Queen,
thankful for this not-so-small
gift of beauty,
my hand
outstretched among the men.

Waffle House

They sit on street corners,
little brown-box buildings.
The best presents come in gold trimmings.

Birthdays, straight A's,
sometimes after church, we'd go,

Dad swinging open
tinted glass doors,
the sublime salivation of bacon,

a tight orange Naugahyde booth,
a rag-wet table, menus jeweled with goo.

Only years later did I know we had no money,
spoiled in gilded nectar from trees,
tin-handled buckets catching each maple drip.

Surely there was no greater creation on earth—
except beehives . . .
and whales so big
a man could camp in them.

I would have liked to have eaten waffles
in a whale's stomach,
but this was better,

sitting like a sapphire in a little brown box,
the blue hues of my dress pleated
like the Queen's.

No wonder I grew up entitled,
surrounded by such riches:
thin women in ponytails
buzzing in circles,

each arm stacked with bounty,
their hands,
sweet with gold.

Wasps in the Garden

Once again, I am here, my old bathtub,
my old room,

just my brother, my mother, and I
in the old house,
knocking down wasp nests,
cleaning gutters, adjusting septic lines,

opening the door to Dad's workshop—
shut four years ago mid project,
gloves tossed on the workbench
for lunch.

The garden knows he is gone.

And we, the hub, the nucleus of our world,
the first cocoon,
hexagons of history waxing around us.

It is as if nothing and everything has happened:
years and illness and little pink babies;
our love: new water pulled from old wells,
young wasps in an aged comb.
What honey there is
belongs to our gentler cousins.

We are unpredictable, passionate, territorial;
our purpose known only
to God and the slender melon flowers.

Thirty-seven times we must visit them
before they turn into fruit;

we, the striped champions of the paper nest,
bound and bold;
revisiting the same garden year after year;

warriors of the melon, the pear,
the delicate elbow of bean.

Birthday

—sent to Queen Elizabeth on her 90th Birthday

This is when everything changes—
when a poem chiggers under your skin;
when your mind cannot rest from its
overwhelming truths.

This is my wish for you:
for a day beneath the full face of the sun,
your skin drinking in warmth
like the orchid I ate last night,

there on my plate in the hoisin sauce and sea bass,
its delicate petals reaching up
as I pushed it this way and that,
till only the thing remaining was
the flower—
the perfect purple poem of earth and mist.

With fork and knife, I gently severed,
lifted to my tongue,
closed my lips around its beauty,
then chewed,
surprised at the taste of perfumed forest floor.

This is when everything changes—

new beginnings: flowers on cake,
flowers in the hair, flowers on fish,

flowers ground in the gentle jaws of the deer—
beasts that tiptoe in the dawn
stealing bud after bud.

From now on, may florals tumble through your blood,
deepen the iris of your eyes.

May everything that struggles
rise from your darkness like asphodels;

the sun
the sun
father of a thousand purple faces.

Cimarron Herd

I wonder if they know their own mythology,
about Sleipnir or Pegasus;

or their famous:
Trigger
Rocinante
Mr Ed;

or their heroes:
Incitatus
Marengo
Reckless
Traveller.

Together, they are summer thunder,
power;
storm with no rain

as they herd,
rumble turning to clops down town streets;

one hundred, two hundred
in the yips and haws of their drivers,
holding the edges
with their own saddled steeds.

Some insist horses
only know
Fear, Clover, Water.

But one looks over
as he runs.
A Palomino with a white blaze.

I see in his eyes:
horizon,
the smell of his mare
at his flank.

Pentimento

But those artists—those lucky bastards,
see how they turn that dead hanging tree
on the canvas
to a pear tree in full bloom,

or how that tornado tail
was smudged mid-twist,
off the ground.

How many faces did *Mona Lisa* wear?
Was she naked with da Vinci
at Villa Vignamaggio?

Did he go back and cover her bare shoulders
with locks of hair?

I have a few regrets,
but not one of them
is loving you.

At night in my prayers,
every brushstroke is catalogued,

and I say
Sweet God Almighty
thank you thank you thank you.

The *Mona Lisa* traveled with da Vinci
his entire life.
Only he knew when he finally
limned the right face.

I regret never seeing Elvis,
or telling William Stafford
how he changed my world.

I regret not asking my great-grandmother
more questions,
not being brave enough
to barrel-race.

I have no repentance
for hours at Audubon Park with my babes
while clean laundry snow-piled the sofa,
and grease welded the skillets;

and there is not enough paint
to cover my every sin,
or to silver chains
over my opened mouth.

I work and rework these lines
like an open palm;
nothing to repent,
nothing to regret.

Tomorrow morning, with you,
the love line
will stretch deep across my hand,
and I'll wake with a wanton half-smile
across my face.

Come What May

June arrived with the wind—
sweatered and booted,
clouds like ghosts
swirling mountain roads.

I always expected home to be
where mother lives, memories
thick as mesquite in open fields,
mockingbirds like summer bullies,
sticker-burs of my DNA
deep into bare feet.

But something is surfacing;
history knows no surrender.

In 2012, beneath an English parking lot,
Richard III was unearthed—
the last English King to die in battle;
his bones whispering the horrors of war—
dead at thirty-two,
eight of his ten injuries just to the skull.

I think of him tonight
as I travel in a vehicle undreamed of in 1485,
to a place I choose to live; choose to fight for;
mother in tears on the phone.

I tell her there are things out there
greater than us all—
people and lives and adventures
burning for divination.

This is my truck.
These are my tires
spinning over the bones of
Neanderthals, Corn Maidens,
Cherokee Princes, Gold Miners.

And I, with the winds of June at my back,
fifth-gear into destiny;
into a kingdom I have yet to name.

Making of a Temple

Uriel hunts in silence
from the mantle.

Angels fold their wings within
painted walls.

Underneath the fireplace stones,
my handprints;
my poetry.

Each tin roof becomes a steeple
beneath stars.

You could bring in the world's wounds
to this cabin,

but at the first wink of moon,
they turn to moths—

somber, sooty butterflies
that disappear
in the dark.

Pearls

It was their way to fight;
their way to attack what came to destroy them—
smooth, bright flesh easing up to the villain;

sitting on his lap like a voluptuous woman,
wrapping milky pink arms; sliding him inside
in disarming, silent surrender.

Death has never known such Beauty—
a curled transformation within pale, opal thighs;
a touch; a gasp; a *pearl*.

Vesuvius

He could blow
any Friday like this,
smoke rings wafting up
between his shoulders.

Since 79 A.D.,
he's roared every 70-80 years.
His time is *now.*
Naples, the Amalfi coast,
allowing no new building permits.

Vineyards and olives flank his shanks,
flowers glory in his ashen dirt;
the poorest of Italy hovel at his feet.

Were he a god,
virgins would be sacrificed;
were he a man,
he'd be Emperor

like Tiberius—
downwind in Capri,
who forced unfortunates
off the sheared leap

all the while Vesuvius watched, yawned,
unimpressed—
he who can change the world
with just a sigh.

Vintage 2014

Another earthquake in Nepal;
the horror, the fear;
a people no longer sleeping at night;

Katmandu rising another three feet
from the darkness.

While in Italy,
the Sun
gently rolls across the evening,
pulling back pink sheets.

The old men say the world is angry,
Wolf Winters in Tuscany—
grapes stretching long toes
deep in the earth,
clinging to heat through winter's white snarl.

So many battled death in 2014,
yet. . . . Sun still rose every morning,
threw open her shades;
swept her porch of stars;
stirred squash blossoms between the vines

while grapes
plumped and shimmied
through heartache,
fire, ALS, flood, cancer, drought,
rape, blood clot, heart attack and quake

for this one moment:
a perfect Sangiovese lifted in *salute*

that we may know
somehow
in some *way*,
it was a very good year.

Cicadas

I have witnessed—
seen them rise like souls
from the cracked backs
of their bodies, pale and soft,
then meditate
as their skin hardens; darkens.

Thirteen years they've waited
for this moment,
to ascend the branches
where they were conceived,

to take a deep breath
in cavernous bellies—
empty as Monday churches—
built to amplify those accordion ribs . . .

and sing a song older than Genesis;
a chorus of roar
rivaling every earthly voice.

Days later, spent and sexed,
they fall in revelations
on those brave enough
to bare summer's scald;

bodies, delicate as communion wafers;
their clear wings,
crystal-thin stained glass;
the magic of hallelujah still inside.

Cape Sounio

I sat on the steps of the ancient temple
and felt the story

King Aegeus beside me on that high cliff
since dawn

anxious for his son's returning ship
from Crete—

White sails would tell the story of *life*
Black sails: that Theseus died in battle

There was a tour going on in Poseidon's Temple
behind me; a thrash of tourists

but I sat with the King as the Athenian sun
began its descent

as the first sight of the ship came into view
the first glimpse of black sails

Then the scurry of dock below, the quick disembarkment
of a son, still cupped, excited with tales

The meeting with two men; the cry of a son
in the perfect pitch of his father

The first fish I ever caught

was a wish;
a dream come true
for a six-year-old,

from a father
who made it happen.

I can't tell you the body of water—
a Texas pond with no name;

but I had a new tackle box
with long wormy pink lures,
and red and white bobbers,
and a package of peanut butter crackers.

And we sat.
And we sat.

And my father talked of patience and timing
and faith.

Faith, I remember mouthing.
It was a hard-toothed word
on my bottom lip.

It was September 28th,
and the fall winds were reborn.

Perch took my bait,
and up he sprang—
glittered and wet

to become yet another lesson
of pumping mouth and gills,
the tiniest of teeth;
the awe of flat faces—
an eye on each side;

and the discovery of *need*—
the sweet urge
to cradle
what had no voice;

to return it
to its secret life
within the murk;
sequins all unseen.

And I walked away,
fascinated
in the slick dazzle of knowledge;

hooked with image and thought:
that strange new silver

to seek
what lives in the silence—
all things that sing
without making
a sound.

Muscle Memory

It's the thighs,
the burn of gluts;
Rock and Roll in the morning;

stepping into a free-fall zip-line.
It's splitting wood in the snow;
the grit-scrape of match;

a full header of bleach
in the hot water cycle;
a chin wax.

Lately, it's been whiskey,
beef jerky,
a cleansing F-bomb,

the iced dive into regret—
into all things tenderized by anger;
into what was never said.

Last night a man yanked my knife
from my boot.
He almost lost two fingers.

Lucky for him,
I'd been chewing
the tin-gum of guilt.

Be warned, I said,
the Blood Moon and I
have a serious thirst.

Phantom Pain

I felt it tonight,
three years out from chemotherapy,
the needle prick in the back of my arm,
the same one as the stomach,
and the thigh;

knowing the pain that followed;
shuddering; remembering
that physical horror.

How is it those sensations
never leave the flesh?
Flashbacks like anaphylactic shocks—

one bee sting too many,
that last chew of shellfish,
the battered body screaming,
Enough!

Warriors know no peace.
They are not *born*, but chiseled
from the rock of terror;
left to battle the masked phantom of pain

that pries open memory—
the nailed windows of nightmare;
knifing muscle, bone, and mind
over and over again;

nightly nursing the fresh bleed
of old wounds.

Margot

1.

She rides shotgun
in her slicker,
green and paling
like these last days of March.

Sleeping in her Chrysalis cradle,
turning
translucent,
into all things sky,

the arc of her wings like stained glass
in the high west wall of Moody Mansion.

2.

This morning,
shine striped the chrysalis tip,
dotted her curves in tiny golden stars;

the constellation *Margot*.
April, the month of poetry and wildflowers
will be hers.

3.

Soon she will pull back her wet cape,
and dry her wings in Spring's sun
as I breathe blessings beneath,

but for now,
I drive while she sleeps:
Red River, Santa Fe, Dallas, Galveston,
Sugar Land, Houston, Denton,
Oklahoma,

both of us holding fast to her branch,
rocking this highway
like wind-blown Sufis,

sure of nothing
but the night sky;
the long thin legs of road.

4.

This morning she changed,
her bright green raincoat now a black pearl,
stars still golden.

I could not leave her:
I took her to the poetry reading.

As I stood before the crowd,
I saw a flinch of movement.
She peeled back earth's curtain

and emerged—
a beautiful origami
of orange and black wings; white spots,

shaking loose all things earth,
drying the wet wings of birth;
quivering as poetry filled the air around her.

5.

I don't know what it means
to witness such magic.

My touch of her, her very first;
my fingers pinching milkweed leaves;

her tiny proboscis uncurls toward my face,
my huge gorgon face
she doesn't fear.

She who died the lowly death;
who felt the black coffin of cocoon,
imprinted light and verse and gorgon.
What could there be to fear?

6.

Two hours later,
fed on the manna of milkweed,
she grew restless,
new wings pumping,
fresh pin legs anxious
for petal and stamen,

she returned to me,
walking the map of my hand;
let me lift her to the redbud tree,
legs reading the soft purple blossoms
of braille,

then flattened her wings,
and let Oklahoman winds lift her
like an offering;

the lope and flutter
of ascending psalms.

Times of Famine

If we could, in times of famine,
call back rent money
spent on shoes passé in six months—
wide heels, flats, new suede booties
ruined in unexpected rains.

Or clothes, still tagged and tossed
in the give-away pile,
or hats we haven't the confidence to angle
across our foreheads.

If we could say to each other:
please don't
thank you
I'm so happy you're in my life.

Have no doubt,
the end of our lives will be a famine
of days; of hours—

no time left
to give the last twenty dollars in our wallet
to the New Orleans beggar with blue eyes,
or retrieve grandmother's pawned pearls,

or put back the stop sign
stolen as a joke,
so one car would stop
the same moment the other accelerates.

In dreams we work hard,
the same vision every night—
our psyche walking backward,
pounding red metal signs
back into the earth,

wondering how the aborted
manifest in ghosts;
if their hungry night howls
will ever let us be.

The Importance of Coffee

God is Calling
so I sit in the mountain sun,

warming my skin
in the cool morning air.

I woke to a rush of deadlines,
to-do lists of the day, the week, the decade,

but God wanted coffee
with cream,

and illumed through the ravens—
the black caws of aphorisms,

then rocked on the porch
until time began its fishtail weave

in and out, stringing memory
and physical pleasure

through each heartbeat
like current through river rocks.

There is light here.
There is rest to be spooned like tonic.

The world can wait
until God empties His second cup,

till Morning relays
her golden baton;

till River loosens
the spell of her song.

Bellitudo Inexpectatus

—for Wesley and Alejandro

There is sweetness in the waiting—
flowers planted,
eager;
faces held up like tiny grails
take, eat, this is my body, my blood.

We wait the hummingbird,
the delicate beast of hollow bones—
the Coquettes, the Brilliants,
the Mountain-Gems.

How quickly shimmer enters our lives
bellitudo inexpectatus;

the iridescence of sudden royalty—
the ruby and emerald,
the oranges, the violet,
oh, the glittering thirst!

Here is this bouquet.
All that I am I give to you.

Always mere hours from starvation,
hummingbirds feast upon the nectar,
the deep-throated bloom
giving life in return;

the trill of wings, a courtship
invoking the holy tune.

There is sweetness in the waiting;
the sudden beauty
of all there is to come.

Prayer for the Women

—for Carver

What power is there in the woman;
lives linked
by the Blood Moon;
the white milk of the dragon.

We are mythological beasts.
Creation flows from the rivers of our hearts;
our wombs.
Each seed yields eight hundred times.

We are power and hunger and need.
We dare men to cast their eyes upon our nightfall,
the bursting leaves of our darkness,
and *not* be changed.

Tonight we stand in mountain daisies and look up;
the cool earth breathing through our toes.

Lovesick elk croon.
Ravens drop blessings of black feathers.

It is good to laugh and drink and cuss.
It is good to hold the fleeting gold of September.
It is good to grow old.

May our hair turn the color of the first sacred snow;
may it glisten in the fingers of the wind.

Blood Moon

The mountain is full of stirring—
the cloven,
the clawed,
all senses pulled by something greater
than any of us comprehend.

In the tree, Cassiopeia first appears—
tiny white-hot fruit
lifting up through the branches,
into the heavens

till she hovers over the river,
over the forest floor,
never once scraping the roof as she turns
upside down in her chair.

Tonight, my birthday
and the blood moon,
a day spent harnessed to cables,
knees bent like Cassiopeia,
zip-lining over
golden Aspen.

Did you ever have one of those days
when a butterfly landed on your arm?

When the sun
and moon
and very earth you stand on
aligned?

When all things cloven and clawed
turned their heads to the night sky
at the very same time?

Marion Morrison

Take it. Try it. I'm not fast
but I don't need to be.

Think pudgy Babe Ruth,
who never had to beat the ball to first base.

Think Janis Joplin,
who never worried with makeup.

Think Minotaur,
with no need to plan the next meal.

It's all swagger, *Pilgrim;*
the perfect hat

tilted just so;
the damn rap of boot on wood.

This is who I am,
on and off—

even asleep, beneath white sheets,
or driving alone,

or crying
beside father's grave.

Take it. Try it.
Eye to eye, good wins and you know it.

It is neither testosterone nor estrogen.
It's the magic swallowed in childhood

that still seeps from the pores.
Call me any name you wish,

make any move you want.
I'm not fast,

but then,
I don't need to be.

On horseback near Bobcat Pass,

a canter
through October Aspen,
leaves adrift in gold snowflakes.

We come to the river,
and Horse
leans her head down between trunks
sliced white
with morning Sun.

I drop the reigns,
lean back;
let all things Earth and Sky and God
have their way.

50,000 Years of Woman

When asked if I believe
the story of Creation or the story of Evolution,
I say *yes*.

I believe there was *nothing*
and then there was *something*,

the theory of synchronicity
and poetry
and the way the fire sparks some longing inside

all the proof I need
to believe a Creator plucked and tucked our lives
for incredible things.

Each morning we put on our face
of foundation and survival,

and stoke those fires
and stir those beans
and tango our babies breast to breast.

What wonders bide beneath the bark of our lives;
nightfall devours each day.

Every evening on our walks,
we gather wood for warmth
and antlers for wit—
a year of deer inside each pale weapon.

We have not come to this moment
in any small way.

50,000 rings of woman circle within.
Let us be legends
a thousand more.

Dog, Dreaming

—wolves and coyotes howl to mark territory
or call others back to the pack

In the high moon night,
the rain fattened to snow,
erasing all traces of man—
cars, poles, roads,

the dark reclaiming
the earth and the river,
the world turned pale
in winter snowflakes.

Coyote came,
creeping close to my windows,
howl yip yip howl
howl yip yip howl

the vigilant ears of my hound
not waking—
but whirled aft,
flattening;

all domestication undone;
called back to the Pack,
his four legs flailing
in a wild mountain Run.

After the Long, Hopeless Night

One bird began his solo,
my open window,
the blue topaz dawn.

One bird began his solo
and the earth and I stirred.

The open window
drinking dawn—
the bottle to his lips.

The blue topaz dawn
a Chianti woman—
Acacia blooms in her hair;

wild fennel sending up their musk
at her feet.

This is the need that could save us all—

the blue dawn
like birdsong in her eyes.

Rooftop Kyudo

One grasshopper, one gecko,
six ants, one beetle,
two grey sentinel pigeons

nesting under roof
floorboards. And yesterday, one
hummingbird questioned

my bright yellow coffee cup.
I look up to see,
high in the windy currents,

an RSVP
of egrets—their crested heads
and immense white wings

skimming eye-blue skies like slow
heraldic longbows,
plumes of arrows, never loosed.

Evening Rooftop

While it hung—that puppet sun
on the pink horizon—

they came without number or name
to feast on dusk mosquitos and flies
and each and every stinging game.

These, my heroes of eve,
my bat-mans and wo-mans.
Who knew?
Who could believe city skies
were so full?

Up I look into an endless horizon—
the night, the space,

neighborhoods of ten million stars
laced together like lamplights.

Do they see this wild flight,
this dive and rise of laughing bats?

On my shoulder,
the breath of constellations—
robed councilors.

I watch them shoot and spur
through blue twilight,
a blur of roughshod burned to dust;

their own shoulders scored
with the white-hot thrust of God.

Prelude to a Swan Song

He couldn't see how Home began to shrink
to House,
how her knickknacks disappeared
one by one
into the safety of dark spaces;
how she never kissed him on the lips.

Driving through Denver,
she passed a church,
a FOR SALE sign in its front lawn.

She understood its loneliness;
the silent cry of wood and stone
after God makes His final exit.

Ventriloquy

What do you say, little one,
before your lungs are even formed,
your heart mining
the minerals of my body
with each pump-pump.

Dig away,
sup my blood,
sup the sunshine sinking into my skin,
the juice of this orange
I squeeze and twist into the glass.

What do you say, little one
about the shape of this life—
such sharp horns in a soft round world;
about others who grew to forget
their mother's voice echoing beneath her heart;
the taste of their own thumb.

Nine months makes a life.
One moment ends it.

Teach me, speak to me,
sing the gastromancy of sifted lullabies
from the lost pockets of childhood.

Yes, yes, I remember hope.
I remember what it feels like
to be wrapped in unflinching arms.

One day you will sit upon my knee
and I will finally understand
the strings of the heart;
the sweet divination of the womb.

Where to Go Among the Chaos

I cannot explain to you
what God is,
that is his job,
if you care to listen,

or how he is in that thin shaft
of sunlight
coming down through the window.

But here is his porch,
among the trestled Clematis
and the Ponderosa pine;

and here is his doorbell
of joy.

I'll leave you now,
to walk in.

Family Crest

If my family had a Coat of Arms,
it would be two minks facing each other,
long furry tails arced in full bush.

In my closet hangs a coat,
long cherished since the 80's,
my name embroidered in cursive
on the right inner lapel.

I pull it out to visit it sometimes
during summers
when I've forgotten cold storage,
running my hands along exquisite sleeves.

I took it on holiday once,
to New York,
suffered insults from vegans
in leather shoes
who never knew how great-grandfather
lovingly raised them;

how he imprinted and named each kit as it was born,
and built them fine wooden cages,
and hand fed them,

how grandchildren serenaded them
in soprano folk songs
as they pet thick pelts
and bonded into espresso eyes;

the great-grandfather who gently kissed each one
as he loaded them into the furriers' trucks;

who fed the neighborhood twice a week
each year during the Depression;

lifting the spring doors of Grace
over each bowed head at the table;
letting loose all resplendence;
each beloved, glossy name.

Moving

I've tossed knickknacks and picture frames
like excess consonants,

rearranged furniture,
hidden drying bras,
boxed stalagmites of books;

stored the shells
and stones of a thousand adventures
in the sanctuary of drawers.

He says it's never looked so good,

but the bones of home creak
as I replace the kids' doorknobs
with the original brass.

Now graduates,
I'll send them
these glass treasures
that opened
every door they ever lived in;

a little bit of constancy in their gypsy childhood.

Tomorrow, I'll dig up
grandma's rose bush,
the one she transplanted
place to place
since 1932,

when each home became house,
and it was time
to move on.

And I think about the first pets I ever knew,
two box turtles—

the way I would sneak them to school;

how in my most burdened moments,
I'd touch their round brown backpacks
through my jeans;
everything most precious to their world
always with them;

how loneliness
bundled
and drooped
when I held them—
pulled away like empty pockets.

How Much Harder the Fight

I take Stafford up in the forest.
He would've liked that.
We sit together overlooking the town,

enchanted by the way Aspen
connect underground—
their sideways roots
holding hands
across the belly of the earth,
never alone; never abandoned.

Mountain salvia blooms,
royal red crowns
among ferns and lichen.

We take the deer trails, Pontus and I,
through the Sangre de Cristos,
mountains still rising from an ancient caldera.

He walks in front,
nose to wind,
finding the downed Aspen—
the crime scene remnants of litter.

And anger scuttles again,
leftover from the morning's paper—
a military boy killed by a gun to his own heart.

I gather the ripped trunk,
drag it back to the cabin,
whittle off its skin,
its eyes of bark,
to the smooth vanilla wood.

This must be the soul of the tree;
the secret sweetness no one could see.

City kids on holiday
can't imagine what it took to lift itself to the sky;
the labor of green leaves;
the golden artist trapped forever inside.

There is no suicide amongst the trees,
just the daily toil for sun and rain and deep earth.

How easy to take a life.
How much harder the fight to live,

though night
burns long beneath us;
though heartache and drought
are sure to come.

Sub-Circles

I put down this book in the airport
to watch.

There is one couple absorbed in a movie
from some small rectangle of technology;
two headsets on;
her head upon his shoulder.

Right now, they could be anywhere,
in any country.
They are lost to the magic of each other;
the art of cinema.

There are worlds that exist within this world—
circles within circles
within circles
like junior high geometry.

It is summer.
They've been to Florida on holiday.
Their shoes are still salted.

This is how all life should be—
the masses flitting; hovering
around a sub-circle

as small as
two touching Atoms;
or Eves touching Atoms—

perfect spooning shapes,
complementing parts.

Her hand moves to the radius
of her growing belly.

We are all mathematicians
with our long divisions
and soul multiplications.

We are one times one,
making one.

She closes her eyes
into herself,
working endless equations;
contemplating the pi of eternity.

She leans further into him;
into his calm,
his one infinite heat.

Waiting. Traveling.

Will these days of travel be counted,
hours on the road or train or air?

Some claim wasted time—
with no clew to help them return—
they pace the floors
with the black soles of business lost.

Let us revel in rest,
or stroll the white stanzas of books,
or put our hand on the warm thigh
of a lover.

God counts all hours.
He will not mind
if the only soul saved this day
is our own.

Tom Clark

I am 98% certain that you, Tom Clark,
poet of "Nux",
are not the same Tom Clark
I went to high school with—

a rodeo man, three years older,
who, as a senior, had already broken
most every bone in his body.

My crush was huge,
and he smelled so good,
and dated Nancy Gidley.

But tonight, I'll let my mind
go down that path
and picture you as *my* Tom Clark,
actually knowing Latin;
a lover now of words;
grey sneaking into those
sandy curled tips of hair
at your shoulders;

your hand, stiff from writing;
your fingers, never quite the same
after that last ride in '82,
bucked off before eight seconds,
your palm crushed
by that old Brahma named Hank;
the one with the busted right horn.

Mountain Doggerel

I open night's window
to the long song of the river—

that opus that never ends;
that sings in fat, snow-melt operas
of cantatas and villanelle.

It must be Aramaic, the language of Jesus—
water, more ancient than blood;
the rune that hums through each body;

some deep muscle memory tune
of lilted phrase and inflection
that scores the hot core
of the heart.

There was a woman from Laredo
translating through her daughter.
She said
she loved my poetry;

said she didn't understand
a single word I spoke,
but could have listened to me read
all night long.

Making Plans

The wind laughs at men wanting control.
It turns to iron,
bullies over the mountain;

crates space in its passenger cars,
windows lowered like cleared clouds
to view the faces of stars—

see how they peek out
through the storm—
wide-eyed children,
every one.

It happened in Vegas—

that eternal vesper tide
of nocturne; sweet purgatory;

men rekindling play—roaming like coyotes
in their best threads, cuffs turned up at the wrists,
the endless pour of spirits,
casting chips and propositions
like the end of days.

Let us lift a glass to the smooth crooners;
their black suits and skinny ties,
that gilded martini age
of dance and patent leather shoes.

And to you visiting Canadians,
your pockets full of lust and bravado,
making women swoon in the verbal tussle of the flirt.

Without Vegas,
how would we know what we're capable of?
Leather pants, glittered nails and eyes that wink like sin.

When I'm 90, I hope I remember
nights at the Golden Nugget,
the prime of our own fifties,
all of us laureled in timeless glory—
not a clock to be seen.

Vegas, where busty is beauty
and men pound their chests
in the grey curls of tobacco.

Croon to me baby.
Nobody tonight is old or sick or poor.

We are all sparkle—
legends in a diner
with a thousand tomorrows,
where the lights are always on.

The Giving

There is no better an afternoon
than to lay beside River,
thin Flies swarming
up and down atop the waters.

Somewhere in this bent bank grass,
Snake meanders through his day.
I see him often—
one thin red stripe along his side.
He eyes Brown Mouse.

He says he does not like
the Woman in me—
he says, like the Minotaur,
he's been unfairly damned
from the beginning.
He says Hummingbird
has a forked tongue too.

But Hummingbird headed
down River, into Mexico,
far above walls and politics,
looking for sugars.

Hummingbird reminds us:
Sky is thickening,
the first Snow due any moment
in flurries, like these Flies.

Trout jumps up and takes Fly.
Snake wraps cool jaws around Brown Mouse.
My floating split-hook whispers,
tempting Trout.

And somewhere beyond Today,
the Minotaur bellows in loneliness,
Cloud rubs her bluing belly,
her young Snowflakes anxious to know

the taste of Wind and Grass,
the warm head of Human and Beast,
the sweet consumption
of River's long tongue.

Banns

There was a promise in him—
an unspoken assurance
in the way he looked at her;
the way he
reached for her.

It was a promise as old
as the Earth itself—
that the green of spring
would rise up from winter's dark;

that the stars,
hidden by the bright of day,
were still there,
beyond the blue,
ever burning.

Dear Ed,

—for Ed Hirsch

I'm here in Marathon Key
and just finished reading *Gabriel.*
It left me breathless;
in tears.

And as I closed your book,
I looked up to see an iguana
in full-armored glory,
spine standing thick as palm fronds.

And I thought about your Gabriel,
how maybe he would have liked
to come back like this—

a creature who, at first,
seemed terrible and fierce,
yet eased his dinosaur body
in full grace
this way and that
into the grass

where he hunted
the tiny cool clovers
between the stalks.

And when he ate his fill,
he climbed up a rock
of grey pitted coral,

and sat on his haunches like a pup,
head up to the sky
in the unnatural stillness
of the cold-blooded—noble,
immortal on his substratum.

And the sun found him
again and again
each time the clouds parted,

as if this was the way life was supposed to be—
the heat, the sea, the soul—
all in its one perfect place.

Ordering Quail as a Friend Lay Dying

I got the message right before I ordered.
Hours away,
I couldn't get there in time.

It was quail, with their frail bones,
and sumptuous meat.

I read about eating the sins of the departed,
but she hadn't left yet,
doctors sure she would pass before morning.

What could one do but pick up the tiny legs
and feast on one so short to this earth.

What could I do but think of her on a ventilator
as I ate to the health of my own body?

I do not know what calls one life to die,
the other to live
from the same disease.

I do not know the mind of God.

But my body says *to eat*; to say grace
over the petite fowl that cross our paths
and fuel our bodies.

Every day there is life;
there is death.
Every day, celebration; mourning.

My friend lay dying,
and I take my wine outside
where meteors heave and shoot.

She would like this.
She would say
Don't stop.
Don't you ever fucking stop.

Red-Haired Descant

—for Maxwell

9:40 a.m.
The wild, red-haired cardinal
began its descant

and I knew her soul had passed
through one bird body
into another.

Where is she now,
besides the oleander outside the window,

flitting leaf to twig,
sharp-singing about the change in gravity
and desires,

and the way the air feels
when you spread your two wings
and let go.

From Liberty to Marianne

—With love to the people of
France, 13 November 2015

Of course I would come, Marianne, we are Sisters.
And the Children of our Sisters are *Ours*.
We have taken them to our breasts,
shared our beds, taught them kindness.

Into the ground we bury our Nieces, our Nephews;
we remember their laughter,
their young gumption to live the way
they wanted too—on *their* terms.
Oh, that we all may live on in their bravery!

We were young once, Marianne.
Our mother, Eleutheria, taught us well:
freedom is won with the armored hand of charity.

I, your younger, wear your same Phrygian cap,
your same Greek robes.
We walk the same morning trails with our great thinkers;
sing the same lullabies to our homeless,
cry over the same graves of our fallen.

Here are my arms, Sister.
It is the woman strength our nations need—
the remembrance of tenderness,
the willingness to take up the sword
to defend our own;
to feed from a warm wooden spoon.

Terror cannot take neither heart nor love.
Let me pass back the torch for you to hold a while.
Let your Children see the endless light
no darkness can dampen; that no evil can befall.

I will stand in your doorway, Sister.
I will watch over the labyrinth of your garden.
God gifts even the roses their armament.
Woe comes to the thieves of the night.

That Bird Out There

Every morning I heard
that bird
out there,

that tiny singing spleen;
body
of mere counted feathers.
We know
its humbling frailty, its
hunger;
happiness pulling up
sunrise.

But I knew one—won at
auction,
a yellow bird no one
wanted,
a vibrant beauty who
spit, hissed
every time we neared, no
matter
how tender the offered
morsel.

I don't speak bird, but I
savvy
sadness hiding behind
cribbed rage—
that wee beating heart heard
that bird
out there,

discontent with tv,
canned food,
and tiny trapezes.
One day,
I unlatched his wire cage.
Instant
was the beauty—yellow
dawn wings;
the sudden song I heard
that bird
out there

The Woman Who Loved Asterion

Every day I give the tour,
each door of this house open
but one—

locked in the attic,
its only key pendulating
between my breasts;

a room only visible from the street
at night,
one lone candle burning on the desk.

On late rainy afternoons
I stretch and settle in there,
where only one lover has ever been.

Sometimes, still,
I look up to the stars
and say his name out loud.

With just one kiss on my neck,
he could call forth ancient gooseflesh,
my body relinquishing—blooming like rain—

head thrown back, giving its whole self,
becoming the frozen opus
of snow.

On this divan,
weather commenced,
seasons cartwheeled,

Spring budded and swelled,
always circling back to the same glorious
white winter song.

In this room,
the latakia of his pipe
still grey-smokes the mirror;

the papered walls
recorded each uttered
stanza.

And the sheets . . .
oh the sheets,
still,

even still,
shoulder his scent—
the deep, ancient musk of his skin.

Tracking

All day,
all day,
every day,
we follow the lines,

caretakers of the world,
paths laid out, drawn out.

Ten hours of road to this healing—
to a cabin of salvation,
to stumble up icy stairs
and into a lion's clawed tub—
hot water ready for the taking;
a wide bed of white.

There are no clocks, no waiting humanity.

Moon checks in, in the night,
palms cool hands
across my hot forehead.

Sun rolls over, pulls back night's dark curtains.
Ravens alight, linger, caw their wordless song,

and coffee waits, snug and fresh,
to be lavished in boiling water,
pressed into glass, lifting its healing aura.

Some say too dangerous, too remote,
no phones, wild beasts . . .
but even my dog sleeps here.

There is no guilt inside this labyrinth,
just the decadence of morning fires;
grooves of vinyl and long needles
to summon Sinatra.

There are snow prints to be deciphered
and an endless river to pursue.
There are revelations waiting for tongues.

There are the words of a thousand poets
on my bookshelves,

and outside these simple doors,
two Aspen chairs wait in old wooden ruts
for bodies wrapped in quilts—

come come, they rock,
come come
come come

What epiphany in our lives to discover
something has happened here;
something greater than us all
has passed.

Postcards from Vignamaggio

I

What can I tell you of Tuscany?

Swallows flit and dip the pools
for swift drinks
between the floating snows of cottonwoods.
They tumble the evening air for mosquitos.

At every turn, vineyards
soldier paths down the hills,
one after another.
I wonder why there is such comfort
in their black-booted clean lines.

There is a spot I like behind the farmhouse;
a chair I pull under the Mulberry tree.

I think of you most there,
wishing for a tree swing—
a double, creaking swing;

trying to memorize the horizon
to relay every detail—
this thirst and yearn for something
half mortal, half myth.

II

Tiny yellow-nose daisies
dot the grasses—
no bigger than the tip of my pinky.

The olive trees stand
stern and still
even in the winds.

The rocks, as everywhere,
have become my friends.

They tell stories older than Homer's—
they who have known human touch
for a thousand years.

I sing to them.
I tell them I want to do for poetry
what Van Gogh did for the stars.

They smile as I touch them with my toes.

III

I grow strong here
with simple food from the garden—
carrots, cauliflower, zucchini;
thin stringy greens like shoots of spinach;
chilled basil and tomato.

The girl with the butterfly tattooed on her wrist
makes a perfect cappuccino.

I travel to Radda for leather;
to Greve for lace;
to Panzano at the Il Vinaio pub
for the best porcini tagliatelle of my life,
once, twice, three times in one week.

There is an old tree that shades its terrace,
and from beneath its wild figs,
I can spot the coral walls of Vignamaggio
miles away.

IV

I have felt the spirit of the wine,
especially the *Mona Lisa* 2006—
an exceptional year.

They've named it for *Mona Lisa* who
lived here in childhood.

I've come to understand
how the wine sleeps;
how it hears every word—
bronzing ruby and deep.
I whisper in its presence.

I feel you like need;
like breath.

V

Fierce is a word I use for buses of tourists
and the blue-headed lizards.
I hear them both when they battle.

There are dozens of ancient fountains
running strong along the roads;
there are flowers and mythological beasts
no one can name.

I've learned
vipers
are always the same color of the sand
no matter where you are.

VI

You are birthing your day
as I bed down mine,
Good Morning, my love;
Good Evening.

I sense you
like lavender wafting
across the open windows:
a savory beauty
even scorpions dare not cross.
I long for your warmth
beneath these white sheets.

VII

I took the train down to Positano,
spent two hours in a gallery—
enchanted by Severino's statue
of the Minotaur
nestling a woman in its arms.

It was you.
It was me.

Time here is different, eternal.
Politics and chaos turn to ash
in the arms of love.

Love—
I'm convinced—
Love changes us all.

Notes

"Kindness:" Talaria – winged sandals of Mercury.

"Politics of the Minotaur:" Clew – Thesius used a ball of thread (clew) to escape the labyrinth after he slayed the Minotaur.

"Politics of the Minotaur:" Oomaka Tokatakiya – "Future Generations Ride"
A two-week, 300-mile horseback ride in December every year from Sitting Bull camp near Bullhead, South Dakota to the site of Wounded Knee Massacre. Done to heal the people. On Dec. 29th, 1890, The Seventh Cavalry opened fire on followers of the peaceful Big Foot— the Miniconjou and Hunkpapa Lakota people (mainly women and children) traveling to Red Cloud in Pine Ridge in the dead of winter to try to escape US conflict. Surrounded by troops, they were ordered to drop all weapons, which all did but one—a deaf man named Black Coyote. There was a struggle to claim his weapon, and a shot was fired. The cavalry immediately opened fire. 350 were killed in less than an hour and left on the ground as a great blizzard came in and covered them all.

"In the Arsenic Pool:" Ojo Caliente – The Ojo Caliente Hot Springs, in Taos County New Mexico.

"Pentimento:" Pentimento – the presence or emergence of earlier images, forms or strokes that have been changed and painted over. From the Italian, *pentire,* meaning "to repent," which comes from the Latin *paenitere,* meaning "to regret."

"Cape Sounio:" Theseus sailed to Crete to kill the Minotaur (who was fed virgins from Athens). On his return, he promised his father, King Aegeus, Theseus' battle result would be revealed in the sails. In their drunken celebration, the white sails were forgotten. The King, waiting at Cape Sounio, saw the black sails, and threw himself over the cliff. The Aegean Sea was named in his honor.

"The first fish I ever caught:" Inspired by Mary Oliver's "The Fish."

"Margot:" Moody Mansion, Galveston, Texas.

"*Bellitudo Inexpectatus:*" Latin for "unexpected beauty."

"Marion Morrison:" Marion Morrison is the birth name of actor John Wayne.

"Rooftop Kyudo:" The Japanese practice of archery.

"Ventriloquy:" Ventriloquy – borrowed and reshaped from Latin *ventriloquus* "speaking from the belly." This noun is made up of *venter* "belly, womb" + *loqui* "to speak." Gastromancy - a form of divination involving listening to stomach sounds. The god Poseidon sent Minos a beautiful white bull to be sacrificed in Poseidon's honor. But Minos kept it for himself. Poseidon, angered, caused Pasiphae, the wife of Minos, to fall in love with the bull. The Minotaur was their child—with the body of a man, and the head and tail of a bull.

"The Woman Who Loved Asterion:" Asterion is what the Minotaur was named in Crete.

Acknowledgments

Alaska Quarterly Review: "That Bird Out There"

ARDENT Journal: "Banns"

Langdon Review: "Pearl"

Right Hand Pointing: "Making of a Temple"

TEJASCOVIDO: "Where to Go Among the Chaos"

"50,000 Years of Woman" and "Where to Go Among the Chaos" appeared in the chapbook *Where to Go Among the Chaos*, Texas Women's University, 2020.

"Ordering Quail as a Friend Lay Dying" was short listed for the Gregory O'Donoghue International Poetry Prize.

About the Author

karla k. morton has fourteen poetry collections. A National Heritage Wrangler Award Winner, twice an Indie National Book Award winner, Betsy Colquitt award winner, E2C Grant recipient, and shortlisted for the Gregory O'Donoghue International Poetry Prize, she's published in journals such as *American Life in Poetry, Alaska Quarterly Review, Arkansas Review, Southword, descant, Boulevard, Comstock Review, Lascaux Review, New Ohio Review and Right Hand Pointing.* Her poetry book with fellow Texas Poet Laureate, Alan Birkelbach, *"The National Parks: A Century of Grace"* (TCU Press) is very historic, as there has never been a book of poetry written about all sixty-two National Parks to help culturally preserve and protect them for the next seven generations. Morton was named Texas State Poet Laureate in 2010, is a songwriter, and is a nominee for the National Cowgirl Hall of Fame.

The Margaret Lea Houston Series

The Margaret Lea Houston Series highlights exceptional work by Texas women poets. This series was founded to honor former Texas First Lady Margaret Lea Houston and her contributions to, and support of, poetry.

Books in the Series

karla k. morton, *Politics of the Minotaur*